Nomads, Pilgrims, Troubadours

A Collection of Poetry by David Greshel

Copyright ©2016 David Greshel.
A Neon Sunrise Publication. All Rights Reserved.

Introduction

There's something about the passage of time that gives us pause; that veritably demands a spirit of reflection and contemplation on the choices and events that direct us throughout this journey that we find ourselves on. It isn't specifically life itself – the seasons continue to pass with the same rhythm and frequency, and all of the varied flora and fauna complete their cycles as is their nature. No, for us it is the human spirit that strains against the boundaries of the natural and instinctual in search of deeper oceans to explore that is the driving force behind our desire to analyze and catalog our conclusions. It's honestly a bit exhausting.

The volume you're currently holding is full of these types of recollections and does little in the way of lessening the need to stop and reflect on where you've been and consider just exactly where you're headed next. If anything, I would say it pushes you into the reflection pool regardless of whether or not you're up for a swim and I'm hoping that's a good thing for you.

So - why a title like Nomads, Pilgrims, Troubadours? Well I think it represents the legs of the journey we've taken on. We all start out in the place of nomads wandering through life, make our way into the realm of the pilgrim earnestly seeking out truth and revelation, and end in the role of troubadour proclaiming the message we have for the world in one form or another. The length of time we spend in these phases varies from person to person and we might often go through them multiple times as our lifespan stretches on. Humanity at its best is unceasing in the quest for knowledge and enlightenment – no matter what the lowest common denominator might showcase.

I also just thought those words would make great headers for the sections of the book.

It might not be what I originally envisioned, but I'm incredibly happy with how this book has turned out and I'm hoping you'll feel the same way. Somewhere in between these words and phrases is a feeling...an emotion...an epiphany meant just for you and it's waiting to be discovered.

See you where the sidewalk ends...

Acknowledgements

There are a lot of people that helped make this book a reality. Sure, I do the fancy creative part and string words together into sentences and phrases that sometimes rhyme and occasionally even make sense but it's all just a writing exercise if I don't share it with the greater world at large. To that end, the following people and groups have been indispensable and a true blessing in my life:

My family - who have never stopped being an encouraging and loving part of my life, even when I'm sure they must think I'm slightly crazy at times.

My City of Refuge Melbourne crew - I found a church that embodies community and is a true example of the fact that your family isn't always blood; Thank you for being there and for going on this amazing journey with me.

The Instagram writing and poetry communities at large - Thank you for the encouragement and feedback on the work I've shared. I've met some incredibly talented writers through these communities and the commentary and exchange of ideas has been invaluable.

All of my friends - you're all amazing and such a blessing to the world at large. Thank you for being a part of my life and for providing me insight and feedback. You're a true inspiration and keep me plugging away at this dream of being a writer.

Readers new and old - if you're holding a copy of this in your hands or reading it on your tablet or phone...Thank you!! I truly appreciate every one of you and hope that you find something to hold on to within these pages...that there's a hope to carry on and that you find the light that never goes out.

David Greshel
October 2016

Nomads

Chamber for Rent

Woke up in an abandoned hotel to the
Chimes on the decrepit grandfather clock
Signaling 2am's arrival and the assault
Of this measured insomnia

They told me I'd find ghosts
In this forgotten place
But the only spirits haunting me
Are whiskey and your memories
Familiar specters I can find
On any barstool in this beach town

Stepped into the half hidden moonlight
Creeping past the cracking shutters
Silver lines dancing in the dusty shadows
Playing at creatures and devils in a lurking
Game of tag with the chimeras in my mind

Why am I here again?

Wandering well-worn paths
I've tread ad nauseam
In search of different answers
In the same ancient routines

Why am I here?

Clinging to some sense
Of imagined normalcy
And the misplaced hope
That you'd finally see
A chance for us to be

They told me I'd find ghosts
And I suppose it's true enough
I'm a phantom searching for
A little peace in the shadows
Your light left behind
In your passing

The Monument of Indifference

A teeming mass of shallow indiscretion
Piled low with pre-furnished expectation
Shared starvation building rank and file simulations
Based upon shattered notions
Long ago forgotten

Shaped and forged in the heart of mediocrity
Keeping pace with overworked automatons
And the dreaming leisure suite
Watching the smoldering characters rise
Blasted and hewn into average stones
The tired battle cry of our mounting apathy

"Meh."

Ishmael I Am Not

I lost sight of the horizon long ago
Suspended in the mists of twilight's gaze
And desperately seeking a glimmer of starlight to point the way

Nothing seems like more than what I've been given
And those that surround me seem to think
There are answers to be found in my keep
Solutions to the conundrums plaguing their existence
That one moment of clarity to illuminate it all
And divine inspiration for future endeavors

The tiniest pangs of guilt gnaw at my thoughts
Knowing I have no clues or theorems to present
That might validate their following...their devotion

Still I press on
Lashing sails and steam
Chasing my own white whale
To the pits of hell and beyond

Dragging these poor souls into the wretched gale
Of my arrogance and pride
Drowning in the self-inflicted torment
Refusing any consolation prize
And lying to myself
When I say there was never another way...

All The Words

"My tongue's the only muscle on my body
That works harder than my heart"
In concert with my lips and mind
Holding in the words I want to proclaim
Simple phrases and sentiment
I'm dying to share with you
Yet the silence seems to echo
As every tiny rationale screams
Through my head
Rattling off all the reasons
I should just let it be
And the dyslexic heart
I got from Paul thunders
Its one note song

I'm not exactly Lloyd Dobbler
There's no stereo to carry overhead
But there are a thousand melodies
I could sing to you
With just a fraction of the feeling
Still burning within this heart
Covered in scars and tattooed lines
That cover the cracks
Not perfect but worth more
Than a pen

The perfect moment
That's what my mind keeps repeating
Wait for it
Wait forever
Leaving me with all the words and no one
To speak them to
While my heart screams
'Let me out and you just might
Find out what it means to be alive
For just one day'

And there you are
Just wondering if I might
Ever speak at all...

Magnetic freeform

Life is a thousand moments
You are loved
Through them all
Never stop playing
You are essential to me

Trudge the void
As though under a shadow
Live through a moment
Rain always whispers
Vision of love in a picture
Still has you frantic
To play life essentially
Black and white
Delirious above me
This storm overhead
We sweat to the beat
Next to never
Our friend lazy
Is why I need you today

Go through me
Still life in love
Whispering a moment
Rob the void of a shadow
As though under the storm
These pictures of our bed
Show their essential vision

This is why I need you

Please love me through the storm
And live as though
You still need these
Moments to never end...

Picture a thousand visions
Still never lazy
Essentially a whisper
Void and delirious
Love in need

One more day
To wonder
What we really mean
One more night
To chase
The stars we've never seen
One more chance
To believe
We're not alone
In the universal sea
Just one more question
We don't really
Want to answer...

I am the ghost of a better tomorrow...last survivor roaming the wilderness of this afterthought culture...only a glimmer of what I once hoped to be before I discovered it was only a dream...left to wonder if I should interrupt your slumber...or leave you blissfully naive...

you are the deja vu in my every thought...sparkling images invading misplaced memories...the deja entendu of every past line and lyric we've ever sung...dancing there on the tip of expression...just out of view and well beyond our reach...the very post card from the edge of eternity that never seems to make it to this destination...the last words we never had the guts to speak aloud...

When the Mob goes Wild

Irresistible force
Immovable object
I'm the mess
Left in the aftermath
Of their foregone collision
Reassembling shattered pieces
And assuming everything will make sense
In the wake of this thunderous silence

A Metaphor in Amber

These thoughts flicker past
Hung like silent markers
In the ether of imagination
Illuminating idle fantasies
Dreaming of daylight
Hovering just on the edge
And a slip of the tongue
Hesitation lingers
Words tattoo permanent
Escape my lips unbidden
But not unwelcome
And this life on pause
Finds solace in the realization
That failure is simply
Never trying at all

Dancing Between Death and Dream

Sanguine transmissions
Echo through the obsidian deep
Immortal in this stygian night
Subtle as the whispered desire
Hanging on trembling lips
Flush with ferocious intent
Appetites primed to devour
Spirits bared for consumption
Hollow cavities the remains
Left as peculiar trophies
Fading in the liquid embers
Of this sunrise Gloriana

Dimestore Cowboy in Suburbia

Sum total of zero experience
And infinite imagination
Equals unparalleled
Wishful thinking mixed with
Tongue-tied first impressions
Leading to long walks
And short piers
Quite a few cold beers
Warming up a barstool
Like a consolation prize
Never quite managing
To fully capture your eyes
And left humming to myself
About late nights and last rites
In the breathless indigo
Of this summer sojourn
Amongst the faded valentines

Asphyxia in the Color Blue

Ethereal phantasms
Plaguing this crowded soul
With tremulous machinations
And half-hearted daydreams
Gasping for shallow breath
Sinking in the glacial waves
The stark rushing panic
Of imminent expiration
And the eternal shadow

Vision snapping back
Bolt upright
Sweaty sheets
Morpheus cedes the kingdom
To Nightmare's calloused grip

Merlin in Vegas

Fragments of illusion
The spark of misdirection
And the gilded mirth
Of oft remembered youth
Bleed into the oncoming now
No psychedelic sorcery
Can ever quite contain
Such subtle notions
Left and leaving off
Synapses flickering
Alive in the grand finale
And the dream becomes you
Precariously balanced
Between ordinary and divine

Lunch Over Sarlacc

Stilted and split apart
The always open maw hungering
For the salted wounds
Long left untended and swollen
Every faded drop of blood
A word on ashen pages
Every striking lash
A line in this self-styled epic
And the longer I lie here
Bleeding out in endless throes
Of spectral musings
I wonder if you've ever
Really seen me at all
Or if I'm just entombed in your
Vain imaginary menagerie

Money and I Don't Even Know It

Such unstable plot devices
Filling these painfully neurotic monologues
I surround myself with
In these moments of loathing
And incisive self-reflection
Carefully staged insurrection
A revolution in royal blue
Overwhelming every notion
I've ever had of breathing
Since the tantalizing moment
My name tumbled from your lips

Mirror, Mirror

A single second hangs
In the breeze unsung
Momentary reflection creeps
In pulsating waves
Hovering just beyond thought
Like tiny swirling eddies
Lapping at the shoreline
Only to slip back slowly
Into the indigo deep
Blink and it's gone
Passed on over and out
Fading into routine
Leaving nothing but doubt

Kalima's Got Nothin' on Me

The ever present question
Floating in the midnight deep
Persistently prodding
One might even say taunting
Pressing ravenously
Until I tear out my own heart
Beating bloody brilliant
Tattooed scars
Frankenstein sewing job
Lifetime of love and loss
On carnival display
Come one, come all
See the impossible man
Held together in hope
And the promise of dreams

Float Like a Butterfly

Enthralled ascension sways
Captivating in secret rhythm
Telegraphed stick and move
Bound to every sliding step
Flexing momentary distraction
In between swinging seconds
Spinning around faded dials
With well tread clicks
An auditory roadmap
Calling me homeward
In the lightning's flash
And perception unknown
Revealing enthralled ascension...

No Strings on Me

Sparks erupt
Flashing tongues of flame
Ignited in exhalation
All this vitriol parading behind my guise
And I am sadly ignorant and mute
Strung up marionette
Dancing ventriloquist
My teleprompter vocabulary
Vocalizing discontent
And all this trending manufactured outrage
In nothing more
Than chains and iron cages

Round One, Ring the Bell

Distance looms in vague ideas
Apparitions foreshadowed
In the growing chasm
Stretching between us
Like the widened yawning jaws
Of near mythical leviathan
Prowling the limitless abyss
Driven by misunderstanding
And the maddening egotism
Rising in thunderous fury
Refined and distilled
To balance on a single glaring
Inflammatory diatribe

"Yeah but what about me?"

Strutter on the Turntable

Spun out and shook down
Reeling in the sweltering sun
Inhalation compromised
Caught in my throat
Thousand pounds of disbelief
Set squarely on my chest
Pressing every former notion
To dust and ashes
Floating out into the breeze
Scattered to atoms
In the wake of your passing
And it gets me every time...

Hello Insomnia My Old Friend

Silence in the infant hours
That creep into morning
While the waking world
Engages in its ritual slumber
Birthing effervescent dreams
And pallid nightmares
Scarcely able to distinguish
Which regularly visits
Eyes wide and glued
Held fast by spinning blades
Reflecting on rotations
Nowhere near the endless
Or the fleeting realm
Aching for relief...release...
The somber sweet embrace
In the arms of Morpheus

Evenings in Python

Torn myself asunder
Every miniscule molecule
Screaming blue murder
Awakened in the aftermath
Under auspicious circumstance
That breathes...bleeds...
Incinerates...feeds...
Delicious irony detonation
Explosions in pigments
Long lost to obsidian seas
Crash landing imminent
Every constricting anxiety
Coiled snug
Begging to squeeze

Count Melodrama and the Ghost of Irony

Still spirits inhabit the ether surrounding me in the dead of night...not much for haunting in the age of technodramas changing attention spans in split second shifts of perception...ghosts of yesterday and specters of some faded tomorrow...all the thoughts I keep between the synapses...these words I never speak...

Matches, Meet Gasoline

It's the way the subtle tension hangs
Suspended in unspoken anticipation
Dangling deep within contested desires
That pulls me out to sea in rip currents
Of ecstatic lust and inebriated love
In a stream of consciousness conversation
Tumbling out of trembling lips dripping gold
In every flirtatious line that garners
A girlish giggle and a welcoming smile
Speeding ever closer to momentary decisions
And last call divisions

She's a consuming blaze waiting to ignite
In the lingering taste of whiskey cherries
Prolonged in passion's kiss

She might reduce me to a forgotten heap
Of disintegrating cinders and ash...

...but oh,
How she might just spark me
Into a neverending inferno

Snowstorms in June, or Just the Imagined Winter of Malcontents

Frozen

That's the sort of shallow term
That gets bandied about to oversimplify
Her current level of emotional output

Ice Queen

An attempt at a curse on the salty tongues
Of every little boy that pressed their luck
And felt their practiced lines derail
On her razored glacial wit

Avalanche Annie

That overwhelming sense of anxiety
Heaped upon her self-imposed exile
From all those endless possibilities
In fear of one more shattered dream

Forever Alone

The kind of slogan she adopts
To garner another round of sympathy
And a celebrated place
Among the other loners all together

And I just sit here in this patient pinwheel
Fanning struggling embers
Beneath the iceberg in her chest
In hopes of resurrecting the remains
Of a tattered heart
With a final look at this love's
Eternal embrace

Memoirs of an Emotional Vampire

I claimed to be an unending desert
With all the bravado of a raging sandstorm
Sweeping every last remnant away
In need of some special touch
To hydrate this arid soul

And for a time I was exactly that
Absorbing all the emotional moisture
You saw fit to give
Even that which you couldn't
'til eventually there was nothing left
And you were the same spent empty husk
Staring back at me
Hollow and dying

Turn the page and this chameleon
Shifts in the shimmering mist
And active camouflage unfolds
In search of the latest prey

One more soul to devour
One more live to live

Which is Worse, the Build-up, or the Aftermath?

There's a sort of underlying pattern hidden deep beneath this maze
Of myriad emotional expressions etched in ethereal extensions
Spilling out in ways we often dare not fathom in the dying light
For fear of never being able to dam the onrushing flood
So we cram it all back inside
Ravenous demons trapped in gilded bottles
Seething...pleading
Waiting

'Do not open 'til Doomsday'

Dying in the Midst of Imagined Immortals

Eyes wide open in the blaze of afternoon
Retinas reflecting a fractal rewind
In scorched corneas
And desert-worthy tear ducts
Void of saline relief
Until nothing else remains
But the full thunder eclipse

What else could I really expect
After a lifetime spent staring into your sun
Desiring a devoted place among the blind?

Something About a Clever Comeback and a Frozen Hell Heart Attack

If it were a simple resignation
To the underwhelming manifestation
Circulating through tired contemplations
That result in shallow indignation
Then I just might accept this speculation
Suspended in the mouth of accusations

Swallow down this anxious indecision
Forever burdened by digital derision
Molded in the guise of misspent passions
In the swollen sallow light of incision
At the expense of a lost persuasion
Espousing the futility in possessions

Listen Jiminy Cricket You've Got it all Wrong

Screaming through the gossamer reaches
In the invisible ice of the upper atmosphere
Falling...always falling
Passing into solitary airspace
Designing cloud shapes with alien precision
In the wake of my descent
Eliciting wishes and hopes
On misplaced heavenly bodies
Without even the power to alter this flight
Or the inevitability
Of this impending crash
And certainly no control
Over the mystery of any life
Beyond my own

I've never been your shooting star
But I'll forever be remembered
As the man who fell to earth...

Laments Disguised in Improv Routine

Be honest
If only for the moment
What exactly do you need
To truly know this is real?

An undying profession?
I'll scream untold devotions
'til my vocal cords burst

An immortal token of affection?
Moon and stars and the world on a string
Or just the ordinary diamonds and pearls
Would not be out of reach or undeserved

An undeniable sacrifice?
I'll tear out my own heart
Store it in your glass display

Be honest
Do you even know?

Or do you just expect me to stand here and bleed...

Are You Ever Gonna Pull The Trigger?

Empty vision staring
Into darkened corners
Out of focus
Listening to the predictable
One note rotation of spinning blades
Synchronizing mental metronome rhythms
Exercising self-hypnosis
And wondering just how often
You lie there staring at the ceiling
Lost in thoughts of me
And wondering just how often
I lie here staring at the ceiling
Lost in thoughts of you
And on and on
Ad infinitum
Ad nauseam
Stuck in the same cycle
Waiting for the needle to drop
And the movement to finally begin

Golden Tickets and Silver Chairs

Wrapped up in the wonder
Spilling out from within
A simple solitary pleasure
Overwhelms these faded senses
Numbed by existential ennui
And radial repetition

Imagination explodes in the wake
Visions of fantastic beasts
Wild and majestic
A dream of ancient life
Unfettered by modern restrictions
In this fabled menagerie

Fade to black
Title crawl in reverie
Ode to a forgotten fantasy
Left between the pages
Lining the cutting room floor

...and Just Look Where All That Planning Got Me

I was prepared for anything
Calculated every eventuality
That might unfold in clever plot devices
Dissected each scenario
With forensic insight
And a coroner's delight

I played through every single
Unwinnable simulation
You were my Kobayashi Maru
A challenge long denied
At the expense of subtlety
And sleepless repartee

I was prepared for anything
Until our lips collided
And a galaxy exploded behind my eyes
White hot and all-consuming desires
Reducing all these careful machinations
To a sideshow carnival ride

Tumblers Today and Other Experience Points

Whispering mist lingers in the waning evening dusk
Maintaining an illusion of mysterious conception
Bent on delivering the rebirth of imagination
In the crack of dawnlight that shatters new horizons
And vanishes in the soaring summer heat

It should be such a simple proposition
Backed with irrefutable equations
And static mathematical proofs
Yet all that seems to surface are the hazy waves
Of ephemeral philosophy
And the constructs of political hanging trees

Spent so much time searching for the keys
But no one mentioned all the locks had been changed
And this skeleton is fresh out of fingers

There's no Safe Word in Crimes of Passion

Someone must have had designs
On a surreptitious acquisition
Of another heart in a mason jar
Like a conquered trophy on display
In the annals of carnal success

It's the only line of reasoning
That could possibly explain
The scene stretching out before me

Where wounded lovers run
To the arms of lustful strangers
Seeking retribution
For passion's excesses
And the devastation of infidelity

And the world sinks into deeper shades of red
Flush with the deepest heat of rage
And I wait for the inevitable detonation
Of this ignored emotional time bomb

Riding Shotgun with the Grievous Angel

Open blacktop stretching out
Carving through barren desert plains
An empty straight line pointing west
On a faded yellow map
From a far less pointed time

Top down convertible chariot
Interrupting the silent reverie
Hula girl on the dashboard swingin'
Gram Parsons on the tape deck singin'
A lonely song about truckers
Kickers and cowboy angels

And all those empty miles take me back
Time travel on the wings of a stereo
To something truly simple
An innocent idealism on full display
Before the subtle deception
In the promise of experience
Carried us all away

The Pitfalls of Sober Self-Medication

Explosions of color
Assaulting late spring mornings
In a flurry of violent pirouettes
Around these black and white constructs
That line empty city blocks
Awash in silent contemplation
Just before the sunshine curtain call
Breaks the daylight opening act
Into hollow reminders of former glories
Painted on tired faces
Hellbent and whiskey bound
Another excuse to slouch forward
Towards the open arms of Gomorrah
And the lilting siren song
Of one more voyage
To the fading outskirts of memory
And the promise of a self-induced dream

Alarm Clock Deathmatch, Monday Edition

Monday morning shades of deepest blue
Washing over weary watercolor palettes
In step and time to the insistent alarm chime
Rumbling in the aural atmosphere
To greet the rising solar waves
and announce the promise of another day
Bursting with unspoken potential
And the marching grind of workday concertos
Competing for undivided attention
To the devil in the smallest details
Left undone and unresolved
In favor of unrequited love

Just five minutes more...

Pilgrims

Aurora

What stars illuminate this horizon
Pale within my vision and shimmer overhead
As the spectrum wavers and shifts
Like floating phantasms reaching out
In astral communications from some
Distant void

The cold fingertips of winters past
Paint the landscape in icy white
And grip these frozen hours
In a quiet stillness
Only interrupted by the ragged sounds
Of ancient ritual

Measured silences hang in the ether
Punctuated by imagination
And the disembodied voices
Of these long forgotten gods and ancestors
Desperately seeking someone who believes
The sky is falling

Ancient commune
Astronomical phenomenon
Messengers of the gods
Solar waves in flight

Perception is such a tricky beast

"Any Colour You Like..."

It hangs there
Suspended motionless
Above the well placed words
And punctuated metaphors
That moment caught in
The space between breaths
A pinpoint of certain knowledge
Unwelcome
Unasked for
And so unlike anything
Ever hoped for
One could ask if it
Can exist beyond here
Or does it simply vanish
Upon exhaling
Dematerializing
Into the ether
Surrounding your thoughts
Yet pounding like the fevered
Heartbeat crashing in your chest
There is no reversal
No option not to know
No chance this last glass
Will erase the moment
Or somehow alter
The outcome
Still it might color the night
And bring a shallow respite
Before the whispers of Morpheus
Carry you off to sleep
Dream into the endless
And let its charm entertain
A smile
There is no night that springs eternal
No sadness bound to you
In chains
There is a sunrise approaching
And a new dawn awaits

Bitter Sunshine

Strange winds whisper
This early winter day
Begun like so many others
In this long December
I wonder what thoughts filled
The early hours while lucky charms
Waited for the cold splash of 2%
And the bacon sizzled on the skillet
Visions of blinking lights and special ornaments
Among the boughs of that Douglas Fir
That heady pine aroma wafting through the room
Inspiring daydreams of tearing through multicolored packages
And joyous exclamations of
"How did Santa know?!"
Bus rides and car trips
Heading off to class
"Did we have any homework?"
"Miss Wormwood, Calvin threw spitballs at me!!"
"Is it time for lunch yet?"

I can't imagine any of them thought about
The thunderous echo of gunshots
In the hallway leading to the cafeteria
Or whether they might be fast enough
To get away to safety
Is Hide n' Seek now survival training?
I'll bet they never gave thought to the notion
That some of their friends wouldn't get to see the winter break

Or that they might not even get to dinner
Spilling out into the daylight
Awash in bitter sunshine
How do they continue on?
How do we explain to all these anxious parents
Such a mindless tragedy?
I have no clever words to say
No easy song to sing
I can only offer shared tears
And grieve into the looming night

On Becoming Lioness

The darkness hung in between
The silence and the scream
Tendrils stretching out to strangle
The flickering light in the guise
Of improvement and "love"

Time seemed glacial
Creeping progress measured
In tears and self-realization

Sparks fly

The suffocated light
Refuses to be extinguished
In the icy depths of
Insecurity and control

It never goes out
Never gives in
Fights the encompassing black
Until it smolders and blazes
Erupting from such beautiful eyes

Unwilling to endure such sadness any more
And the sound of her voice screaming out in the night
Beckons the sunrise and the arrival of dawn

This time won't be like any before
The air is electric and she's ready to roar

Still Life on Pause

Darkness creeps in
Slowly overtaking the edges
Of the half-light
That dimly illuminates this room
Eyes wearily roaming the walls
Scanning the ever growing shadows
And listening for the mocking whispers
Of scheming serpents
Seeking that oh so perfect spot
To sink a scarlet blade
The second your back is clear
That stress hangs heavy
Weight like a millstone
Threatening to drag you under
And it almost feels worth it
To just stop struggling...
But what would that accomplish?
Don't let it slip away
Don't relinquish the fight
Hold on to that sliver of hope
And remember
"There is a Light that never goes out"
And it will shine again...

Shine On Starlight

The crack of the horizon spread
As the sunrise deepened the morning
Splitting the sky of pink and amber
From the deepest ocean blue
Daystar slowly lifting
Reflected in the rippling waves
Cascading on the shore
The salty foam running rivulets
Between your toes
Submerged in sandy crevices

Listen for the click
And the snapshot is secured
Preserving this moment
In pixelated glory
Frame of reference
For the coming brushstrokes
Paint meet canvas
Imagination unwinds
And art emerges
Amidst the lunar illumination
That beckons the heavenlies to dance
Shine on starlight
And dream for me
Once more

Where the Heart Is

Nightfall tends to bring reflection
Ruminations on the eventful day now past
Fill your thoughts while you sidle down the hall
Were all things quiet on the western front?
Did the emergencies storm the gates?
So good to have this quiet refuge to retreat to
This house full of love and laughter
Adrift in a sea of memories
And a little welcome mystery
Somewhere in between

The sound of distant starships
Echoing a far off galaxy long ago
Are not foreign within these walls
Often accompanied by the wail
Of thunderous guitars

So many pleasant experiences
Yet still a temporary abode
"Home is where the heart is"
And someday we will finally
Cross over that threshold
To find eternal rest in the Son

__Two Years, A Lifetime__

Caught a breath
Just hanging in the ether
Suspended in the moment
The world spun away
An errant top gliding
Through the wreckage
Of these in-between days

Time heals all...
But no one ever defined
The measurements
Seconds, hours
Weeks, years
A lifetime...

Two years to never
Getting any easier
Living in the small moments
Where we still feel your touch
Hear the whispers of your love
Knowing that you're only
A stray thought away
Yet the distance is consuming
And the looming sadness
Is often deafening
Still we try to dwell in the
Good times
And pleasant remembering
Knowing you'd want
A smile and a laugh

So for today
We'll say
Heaven is here
And we're beside you

...just like any other morning
Here in this dream
Of Avalon

Something Like Breathing

It starts in just a small moment
Yet there is nothing quite so amazing
Followed by several months of weird cravings
And mood swings in a slingshot swing-set
Until the day finally breaks and you wonder
Was this worth it?
Is this pain the end of me
And will I ever make it through tonight?
The sound of that small cry
Erases every other thought
And the sight of that tiny face
Answers all those nagging questions
Leaving the biggest smile amidst the glint
Of sweat and tears.

The days begin to accelerate
Watching a growing child
And wondering when your precious little one
Got so grown up
Peeking in on them in the night
So peaceful in their dreams
Even something like breathing is still magical
While they slumber

All the special events
Begin to blur
First days, first loves
Graduations and weddings
Anniversaries and children of their own
So many things to see
Experience through the years
A lifetime to be proud of
Despite the hard times

And that child will think of you
In many ways
Through the passing time
Friend
Confidant
Coach
Annoyance
"So unfair!"
Example
But more than any other
You will always be
Mom

If it Wasn't for Fairy Tales...

"To sleep...perchance to dream..."
A thought so simple
Yet often lost
Life moving at speeds
Demanding we hold on
And keep moving

But I like dreams
And a pace that beckons
Us to sit and ponder
And take the time to wander
Somewhere we've never been

"If I lay here...if I just lay here...
Would you lie with me..."
And stare out into the stars
Counting streaks across the night sky
Making up stories about
Intergalactic travelers
That take each step towards
"Infinity...and beyond"

If I asked
Would you dare to wonder
What it might be like to swim
The deepest reaches
Looking for lost clown fish
Riding sea turtles
And just maybe find a certain Mr. Sherman
On Wallaby way in Sydney

Would I see you
Singing along
On a jungle path
Sharing a little hakuna matata
With prospective royalty
And indulging in
A bizarre buffet

Would you come with me
Down the rabbit hole
Just to see how far it goes?

Yes, I like dreams
And stories
They make us feel alive
And the best ones
Are out there waiting
To be discovered

Will you come with me
Dance beneath the stars
Forget all about midnight
No pumpkins in sight
Every good story has
A princess
Who takes your breath away...

And I haven't been able
To catch mine
Since the very first time
I looked into your eyes

Teapot Typhoon

There are days that never seem
To turn out like they're imagined
And too often they outnumber those
That appeared just as they were pictured
In your dreams
But then no one ever promised
Life would be a walk on the beach
Or a downy feather bed...
And if they did it was simply naiveté
Or an unbridled desire
Of the heart against the head

Still this tumultuous living
Being made in the eye of a hurricane
Has such profound moments
Of friendship and joy
Love and compassion
Sparks of overwhelming rapture
And the purest ecstasy
Of a child's laughter in your ears

The tempest will rage and the seas will ever seek
To test the solidity of the vessel
And the mettle of her captain
To the point of shipwreck and despair...
As is the nature of the storm
In its most savage display

Faced with such a fury
It would be so easy to just concede
And let it all be swallowed by the sea...
But it can't rain all the time
And safe harbor is not
A siren's dream

Silent Battles and Weary Soldiers

Nearly gave up yesterday
Felt it all just so immense
The crushing weight of life
Through the fish eye lens of self
Atlas I am not
Never meant to carry it all
Nor am I Sisyphus
Though I'm no stranger to futility
And the doubts and stress that plague me
Make me kin to Thomas
Waiting to see pierced flesh
On the hands of my Saviour

Nearly gave up yesterday
Almost let it slip away
Caught the faintest glimmer
Shining on the periphery
Heard the warmth of hope
Whispering in the breeze
Set my grip and shouldered on
One more day to save

City of Love in the Hands of the Heartless

Thunderclap in a tin can
Deafening in a soundless instant
Stolen breath ripped from sunken lungs
Seconds before the concussion
Shattered brick and bone

Dazed in the emerging wreckage
Every B movie apocalypse unfolding
In the darkness of this anxiety
Exacerbated by sirens wailing
And the staccato machine gun blast
This can't possibly be real

Reality the rudest awakening
Illuminating the coldest sober knowledge
Drunk in the madness of humanity
Engulfed in its hollow depravity

Arm in arm we stand in defiance
Unwilling to yield to such hatred
Or bow to the terror of despair
Fingertips nudging the volume
As we sing along with Lenny
Belting out 'Let Love Rule'

Paris...Je t'aime...

I'm not Vain, but it's Definitely About Me

Why do you write?
What has it ever gotten you?
The kind of questions rattling around
In an already crowded headspace
Unbidden and undesired
The kind of doubt that plagues
Such darkened hours
Meant more for whiskey drinks
And bad decisions
Than the death of dreams
By a thousand cuts

Why?
Where else are all these emotions
Going to flow
When the soul can no longer
Restrain them
Every drop of ink and clicking key
Siphoning the reservoir
Tearing the veil
To enlighten and entertain
And maybe even express
Such often understated longing

It's an exercise in self-invention
One golden word at a time

Chris, I Borrowed a Few Things

Cradled in familiar mattress coils
Winding into a waiting nocturnal embrace
Shifting sands of slumber sleight of hand
Drifting slowly towards the endless dream
Binaural audio accompaniment
Soothing the fraying edges

Cornell paints with Buckley's Grace
Birthing the horizon of a Euphoria Morning
Dawning in the midst of melancholy
And the hint of a hope to carry on
To find the Temple of the Dog

The last notes fade to silence
World on pause in the span between
While the sky cracks and cries frozen tears
Crystalline ivory beauty arrives
And everything is new just for tonight

Part Time Bard on Full Display

"Tell me a story"
She said
Stretched out before me
eyes transfixed in mine
With smoldering expectation

Synapses sparking rapid fire
Imagination interstellar overdrive
Conjuring gargantuan characters
And superfluous monologues
Bound in iconic scenery
Enveloping the devil in the minute details
Spinning wildly between ticking seconds

Tiny spider trails weaving twisted webs
Interlocking plots and themes
Painting verbal murals
And oratory self portraits
Wrapped in allegory and mythology

"Once upon a time..."

Ruminations on Rock n Roll Immortality

"...That's the way I like it baby, I don't want to live forever!"
Echoed out of every pore in your body
Through countless hours on Sunset
Or holed up at the Rainbow
Sweating Jack Daniels
While growling timeless anthems
From every stage on earth

Living embodiment of Rock n Roll
On your own terms with your own rules
Genuinely brutal honesty
Never overshadowed the kindness
Or the kinship found
On the never-ending tour

"Who wants to live forever?"
To borrow another's phrase
Maybe not so much
In the case of flesh and bone
But you are Rock n Roll
And legends never truly die
Forever in our hearts
And in the anthems that remain
Immortal in the songs forever sung

Chameleon in the Company of Diamond Dogs

Look up to the heavens in their evening attire
Shining silver pinpoints illuminate the indigo canvas
Scattered along the everlasting horizon
Recalling a roaring golden comet
And a man who fell to earth
Carrying Martian arachnids
With a message from Major Tom

Flirting with androgynous affectation
A changeling soul imparting heathen wisdom
In the halls of the Goblin King
A labyrinthian undertaking
For Aladdin Sane
In the employ of the thin white duke
Nestled in the shadows
Watching rebels and their moonage daydreams
Tempting china girls to dance

A chill sweeps past
The harbinger of black stars falling
Spilling secrets of life on Mars
And whispering tales of velvet goldmines
Lost to us when you stepped through the door
A hero for all of us just for one day
And it's only forever, not long at all

Royal Seduction in Violet Thunderstorms

We just went crazy in the heat of those sultry summers
Spent cruising to sleepy beach towns
In a crimson corvette convertible
Top down and searching for diamonds and pearls
With the tears of a dove in a raspberry beret
And the soulful solo of a secondhand store guitar
Signaling the announcement of a party circa 1999
In the oncoming dusk enveloping Paisley Park
Where I might just die for darling Nikki's kiss
Beneath the shadow of this graffiti bridge
Where we learned it sometimes snows in April
Though tonight we're drowning in the purple rainfall
And the sober realization
That manic Monday is inevitably on its way
And nothing will ever truly compare to you

No Quarter Asked, None Given

I have to imagine that you thought you were clever
Surely in the very least it crossed your mind
That these situations could be manipulated by design
To satisfy a predatory appetite you meant to disguise
In elevated promises and the slickest serpent tongue
Equating every rising dream of art appreciation
With your lecherous intentions and payola power-trips

There are no shadows to be found now
No shallow holes to hide away
You've awakened the lioness
Ravaged and ravenous
Willing to leave it all as a smoking crater of ash
Before she'll let you prey upon
The next unwary daydreamer
To wander in your snare

Spinning Vinyl Memories Orbiting Russian Circles

I spent the sweltering summers abroad
Expanding my previously limited horizons
With Jets to Brazil via Burning Airlines
On a one way flight to the dying sea
Where we celebrated Rites of Spring
In an altogether belated fashion
Amid subversive Social Distortion
And the unavoidable sounds
Of the Damned on royal holiday
With King Diamond and a pious Ministry
Asleep at the Wheel of the Killing Joke
We have chosen not to accept or believe
In the glory of hindsight deferred
For the vision of Sonic Youth
And the hope of a Daydream Nation

Wheel of Identity, Turn Turn Turn...

If I'm truly being transparent
Leaving nothing to hushed silences
Or creative omissions
Laying bare this naked soul
Exposed in all its excruciating glory
Counterbalanced in blood and ink
Painting memories in tattooed scars
Covering every speck of imagination
A sight no other eye but mine beholds
In the entwined grasp of mistaken identity
Long accepted as my picture of reality

If I'm truly being transparent
I might see this all for the truth it is
Acknowledge just what sort of fables
Masquerade as undeniable facts
And leave me shackled
To an endless circle
Of pride and shame

Maybe it's time to be transparent

Milestones on Forgotten Blacktop

A single light flickers in the awakening
Illumination blurred in the fading dusk
Slowly narrowing to a lone candle burning
At the edge of an unknown tomb

Is this the opening act?
Or the final curtain call?

Collective memories stir in national souls
Awash in shades of crimson, ivory, and cobalt
Proudly singin' Lee Greenwood's song
In unified harmonies
If only for the fleeting hours
Of another memorial day

Temporary as it ever is
We remember all the lives
Laid down in a soldier's service

Honor in the bloodshed
Gratitude in the hearts we fed

Not Much for Endings, I'll Take a New Beginning

There has always been
A comfortable measure of freedom
In the unknown time or hour
Which holds the presence
Of a death angel in flight

Strange how fluctuations shift the pattern
Driving deeper anxious angles
With every new phantom pain
Or inconclusive outcome
Spiking in random repetition
On another hopeful test

The sound feels closer now
Not some imagined distant echo
But the clear and steady thrumming
Of powerful wings beating empty air
On a journey a lifetime in the making

Never one to shrink away
No terror to be found here
Among the possibility of farewell
Just the simplicity of knowing
Every minute is worth it

...Right down to the very ends...

Seventy Two Virgins and Other Fables for Small Minds

I have to wonder
Just exactly what it is
That drives a man to murder
Over thoughtless ideology
Engineered to enslave

What could this action possibly gain?
Does the stain and stench of senseless death
Somehow bring you joy?
You think you're a sort of righteous soldier
Bent on a holy crusade
And other grandiose delusions of paradise
In a less than clever masquerade

We name you what you are
Coward in the first degree

Third Time's a Charm and Other Clichés

I listened for the static cry of white noise
That always seemed to echo in your reactions
To all these shallow suitors trolling for a bite
Like you're some catch of the day
At the local seafood shack

Typical scenarios abound
Almost as if they have cue cards
And tabs from a take-a-number wheel
To signify their hollow intentions
Like you're the prize at the end
Of a carnival game

Still you tend to play along
Entertaining their disheveled attempts
To impress with a gaudy peacock strut
But you tuned out in hours long past
And all you hear now
Is the overwhelming monotony
Of Charlie Brown's parents

Understanding in the Absence of Experience is Nearly Nonexistent

Has it always been this dark?
Alternating shades of ebony and obsidian
Rolling in the waves on this midnight colored beach
Of the desolate island I've long found myself
Imprisoned upon in solitary isolation

It's not that there's no one
I see them floating past with their glory
And their alien purpose
So untroubled by the shadows that surround
These tiny shores

They call it light...a hope to carry on...
And I find myself longing for it desperately
While I bleed to know I'm still numbered
Among the halls of the living
And glimpse the flashes...the heat...

A chill settles in
Creeping through my tired flesh
My aching will
Attempting to eradicate any trace
Of the flickering embers of love

I so very much want to see this light
This undeniable hope you have...
Has it always been this dark?

Observations in the Minds of Don Juan and Cyrano

Crazy how it never seems to matter
Just where in life the moment takes us
Or how many moons have passed
Between the last ones we shared
Or whose arms we last lounged between

There are endless starfields with light in bloom
Waiting to escape to our quiet corner
Of a conscious expanding universe
Waiting to illuminate the dreams
And wishes bestowed upon them
Waiting for this moment
Dawning in the glow behind your eyes
And the radiance of your smile

No one else seems to be aware
Lost in the tangled surface
Strangled in their own lust
Such selfishness breeds only contempt
In the cold flame of your heart

Still smile for me
If only for this moment
Know that I can see the Queen
Only waiting on the undeniable presence
Of her King

Listening to 'Happy Birthday' Echoing in Birdsong

Sunlight sizzles across a darkened dawn
Golden shafts streaking heavenward
Sundering the endless horizon
Splitting earth and sky with another first light
Signaling the demise of another last night

Optimistic reflection fresh in the forethought
Of one more solar orbit occupying the registry
Trying to keep up with this fading diary
That frustrates these scribes and Pharisees
Intent on monitoring every aspect of my ordinary

All of this passes in such silent amusement
Amidst the rousing birthday choruses
Sung in long familiar melodies
Rekindling sweet wishes
And another chance of creating their eternal life

Last Call for All Stops East of Eden

Just a dream we shared
Sounds a bit like farewell
In the resigned tones
You paint your words with
In measured sentences
And plaintive monologues

Funny how the pendulum swings
Predictable, reliable
Almost by design
Like the fables you've created
About misplaced feelings
And my ne'er do well intentions

Are you asking me to bleed for you?
Seeking some sort of sign?
I would drain these veins
And paint these pristine white walls
The deepest crimson love letter
The likes of which no bard has ever seen

...It was just a dream we shared
Your words...not mine...

Well darling the dream is over now

Alive in the Ashes this Wildfire Left Behind

They keep us slumming on the surface
Embroiled in skin tones and broken homes
Too busy trying to eviscerate one another
To plumb the depths of the tortured reality
We find ourselves asphyxiating in

It's so far beyond these crafted distractions
That it would be a hysterical amusement
If it wasn't so damnably tragic
Naiveté in white the very first casualty

Sinister sounds echo in the abyss
Muffled by sludgy stygian shadows
That seek to mask the ghost of imperialism
Screaming a litany of manifest destiny
In a language breeding only death

Noxious vitriol floats skyward
Passing through spin cycle layers
And self-loathing deception
To the starving ears of the masses
Seeking an army of knowledge
But finding only shackles
And a place in the never-ending firing line

Literally Literary and Loving Every Minute

There was talk of less traveled roads
And hidden doorways of infinite perception
Overheard in conversation
Between silver tongued swashbucklers
And bored existential philosophers
Looking for a brave new world
Amongst the accumulated ashes
Of a season spent in hell
Trying to convey the sudden appearance
To the lords and new creatures
Unaccustomed to the sound of furies
Screaming out bloody symphonies
In the uncharted darkness
Engulfing the edge of the map
Where an untold number of monsters dwell
Before the world goes flat
And ends at the abyss
With hope abandoned for all passing through
Looking for the answers
Within these yellowed pages
And an ancient bottle of wine
Pulled from the water
And the hand of a celebrated friend
In such interesting company

Navigating the Many Faces of Inspiration

Sometimes you're the muse

Sometimes you're the song itself

Sometimes you're just the instrument
That put it all in place

Extrapolation of borrowed lines from Bukowski

Spoken enigmas dance
Spilling complications
In a rush of practiced tongues
Painting verbal portraits
Obscuring implicit figures
Opting for muted impressions
Carefully constructed
Balanced in silent echoes
Careening through cavernous
Fathomless fanciful fables

...And we site here puzzled,
"Sifting through the madness
For the word
The line
The way"

Faded Denim Jackets and Newly Opened Hearts

Turned on the battered radio
Tuned to so many distant yesterdays
Back when trouble was far away
And everything felt like the first time
When we discovered whispering stairways
On the wind that was forever crying
Mary's name as billowing smoke covered
The water that ran along the ominous wall
Built by those children of the grave
Residing with diamond dogs in the shadow
Where this daily rocky mountain high
And careful observation
Has ever indicated
People are strange
But we held on loosely and haven't let go
Couldn't stop believing if we wanted to
It begs a smile
And one more silver dollar
It was just what I needed tonight

Nocturnal Royalty on Holiday

Stepping out from the shadowed depths
Draping the cloak of darkness
Around pale shoulders
In the solitary silver beam
Of Luna's gaze
Welcome spotlight
For the reigning queen of the night
Lilting voice
Siren song
Drawing forth nocturnal children
To feed upon the unaware
Mesmerized
Hypnotized
Powerless in her allure
Willing martyr
To the flames of her desire
Set alight
In the whispering temptation
Of immortality

Old Fashioned Love Songs and Boombox Heartbreak

It was a memorable summer
Spent entwined in one another
Not quite like '69
But the boys were definitely back in town
And we lived in the grooves
Between the wax and the needle
Spun round and amplified in every note
Lifeblood dripping off every vocalization
As we sung in each other's ears
Meaning every word
Until the moment we didn't
And it all came to a screeching distorted end
Stuck somewhere between left and leaving
Contemplating the unraveling meanings
Of what jets destined for Brazil might solve
And that's when the night finally ended
With a worn out tape deck breathing its last
Giving up Tom Joad's ghost in silence

We broke our own hearts
Without any sort of excuses asked
And those summer boys
Have long since disappeared
In the midst of the oncoming storm
And the longest winter of our lives

Doodles and Daydreams

Stars fell in icy twilight
Streaking silently against the deepening indigo
Pinpoints of fire breathing their last
To fuel the dreams of imaginations
Lost in the haze of youth

Dreams we often stumble back to
In the overwhelming moments of restless repetition
Wondering how we ended up so far
From these idle fancies
And what it might take to somehow retrace the path
Or shake the sketch and start again

Magic erasers
Second chances
Tabula Rasa beginnings

Never too late to dream...

Hey Francis, I Found Your Mind

Our first thought expands
Unfolding in the patient rise
Of the newly virgin sun
Stretching, growing
Testing the delicacy
Of imagined limits
And playing questions
With the age of reason
Abandoned to the hungering
Savage common sense
Logically emotional
Emotionally logical
The debate is endlessly devoted
To one gnawing doubt
That the beautiful memories
Will ever trump
The pain of might've been

Caught in Phil's Spotlight

Captured in the warm embrace
Of this sultry summer evening
Enraptured in the dying light
Of Sol's sunken farewell
Humming cicadas crooning
The prelude to nightfall
Welcoming the shaded liberty
Of astronomical phenomenon
And delirious exultation
Single shining circle
Beckoning Lynott's waltz
Amongst the shrouded souls
And overgrown tombstones

If They Handed Out Awards for Self-Destruction I'd be a Gold Medalist Every Time

I wanted all of this
Whether I've ever admitted it to myself or not
I set it all in motion
Pulled every string in place
Tied it all together in neat conspiracies
That never intersect with common reality
In even the slightest degree
Maintaining the illusion of camaraderie
Despite the imposition of solitary piety
In this community of necessity

Self-sabotage is an art form
Mastered unintentionally
And displayed with furious exclamation

I Mean, This is a Fairy Tale Right?

There were simply too many variables in play
To know exactly how this chapter would end
Or even which page would reveal the motivation
So desperately longed for...bled for...
And every new player thought they were the chosen
The one meant for glorious destiny and bardic tales
You can see their noble corpses in ramshackle stacks
Lining this decimation highway for millennia
Leading out into the unbridled wildlands
And the desolation of our faceless opposition
That still manages an unnerving grin
And a fixated pair of soulless eyes
Unceasing in their malicious pursuit

...And I devour every bloodstained page
With a ferocious intent on losing myself
Somewhere between 'once upon an time'
And 'they lived happily ever after'

Imagining the End of Casanova's World

It all unraveled in fraying withered strands
Frazzled and faded floating in the breeze
Blowing in the evening chill
Slipping through aching blistered fingertips
The unfinished tapestry of all we could be
Forever came undone

And in the end
Love meant letting go
Releasing the ties that bound souls
Left free to roam
Building lives in the arms of others
Standing on the molded memories
Of might have been
And never was
Treasured in the knowledge
We both will pass this way again

Listening To This Desert Life

Waiting in the entrance
Of sun blistered Mojave
Scorched earth between bloody toes
Exposed in worn out sandals
Desert experience on overdrive
Dreaming of distant pacific shores
And pleading for the relief of oasis

Passed out in the painted canyons
In the arms of coyotes
With spiritual rabbit trails
Courting peyote moonlight
And the questions never answered
At the dawning of the sun

Raptor in Endless Flight

It's the speed that's most unsettling
An explosion of feathers and talons
Knifing out of steel gray skies

Avian assassin tearing into unwary prey
In the dying light of day

Troubadours

Peter

It started with the fish and a spirit crying out
Longing to be filled with revolution and redemption
We'd read the prophets and followed John in the desert
We could sense something was coming
And then He was there calling to us
Asking us to follow Him
We left our nets there on the beach
And wandered off into a new adventure

Three years in and things have been a whirlwind
So many wonders these eyes have seen
And I couldn't even begin to tell you them all
I sometimes scarce believe them myself
And yet I know deep within that everything He's taught
Is the embodiment of truth and righteousness
It strikes me in those moments
The divinity of my Lord
And I wonder when He will finally reveal Himself
To everyone and purge our land of these oppressors

Tonight there's an uncertainty hanging in the air
Covering our somber meal while He talks about his impending death
There is mention of betrayal, abandonment
But surely He can't mean me
Yet He tells me of the onrushing denial
Three times and the rooster song
Steadfast I hold to my proclamation
And we retire to the evening prayer

Roused from our unexpected dreams
Greeted by the forewarned betrayal
By one of our own
Anger and rage welling up within me
And my sword lashes out
To protect my Lord
Yet He will not have it
He continues to proclaim events
Are unfolding as they must

And we all scatter in fear and disbelief
Bringing our dinner conversation
Into the light

I cannot let this lie
Circling back in the shadows
To watch as they take Him
Into the proverbial lion's den
Where hungry jackals wait
To pick His bones with the teeth
Of their envy
Faces coming into view
Questioning me while I try to remain apart
Marking me as one of His men
I deny each one more fervently than the last
And on the third I see His eyes upon me
As the rooster song fills my ears
His words thundering in my mind
Turning away at a dead run
Molten torrents of tears
Carving down my face as my body
Is wracked with bitter sobs

The day drags on and the crowds have gathered
Covering Golgotha to see this execution
My disbelief can hardly be contained
Why has my Lord allowed this to happen?
I can hear the pounding hammer and the throaty screams
The result of nails piercing flesh and bone
And they raise Him up
Hanging on this tree between two thieves
Breathing prayers of forgiveness to the very last
Confusion clouds my thoughts
And we run

Three days in and things look bleak
None of us know what comes next
Our world is shattered
Our Lord is gone
When Mary burst in with incredible news
I could hardly believe it
We ran to the tomb

He was nowhere to be found
And His words flooded in
He is risen...could it be?

Back to the fishing nets, to what I know
Maybe the adventure was just for a little while
But the fish will always be there
Even if none appear to be available for the catch
Yet someone calls from the shore
"Throw your nets to the other side"
Resulting in more fish than can be hauled
And I know my Lord is there
Swimming for my life
In a rush to greet Him
A meal prepared to share
As was always our way
And He asks me of my love and devotion
Three times I answer
And feel the warmth of restoration

So many years have passed since then
So many trials we've faced and miracles we've seen
The revolution we craved but never really understood
Is now engulfing the world
A revolution of the heart and mind
A rebellion against the power of eternal death
Which forever lost its grip that black Calvary day
Our Lord Jesus reclaimed the keys
And restored creation to its rightful path
I am old now and the oppressors have finally
Pronounced my sentence
They are leading me now to that place
And I see the instrument of my demise
Wooden crossbeams gnarled and splintered
Tied and stretched out
Yet I will not let them set me upright
I am not worthy to die like my Lord
Hang me upside down

Pearls and the Price They Bring

Hours slipping through daily crevices
Washed in the sands spun by the tide
Accumulated shoreline fodder
Building up these vacation beaches
Burying the hidden wonders in the wake
Of the passing lunar phases
And left to wonder if anyone
Ever noticed them at all.

Time crept on
The weight of years...centuries...
Immense in their totality
Piled all around
And left waiting...always waiting

Brilliant blinding shafts of light
Scorching in their warming appearance
Suddenly upon me
Amid new surroundings
Lifted forth to freedom
Face to face
Beholding Him
Dirty and scarred
Full of Love Eternal
The one that has never stopped searching
Since the moment Life began.

Short Musings of the Creator

I gave rise to this
Birthed you in a flash of ideas
And the haze of a dream
Spoke these words into flesh
And knew joy at first breath
Your soul sparked and rose
Stretched its wings
And took flight into the gloom
I wonder when you'll seek me out
Desperate for answers
And it hurts me in the deep
To hear you think I never once existed
Or am somehow just your dream

No Orphans in the Kingdom

We all started in the dark
Orphaned and lonely
Scrambling ravenously
Searching such vain ambitions
In hope of everlasting
Satisfaction realized
At the might of our own hands
Crumbling in the black void
With the inescapable revelation
Of such futility

Startled by the appearance
Of electromagnetic illumination
Drawn to the warmth
Of enigmatic epiphanies
Casting off solitary bondage
For the preferential titles
Of Daughters and Sons

Delirium Daydreams

Sparks flash
Igniting the obsidian deep
With a brief showering
Of fiery pinpoints
Illuminating imagined fantasies
Enchanted and ethereal
Anticipation overwhelming
Every stolen sensation

Fading into Mysterious Algorithms

Lying on a sheltered beach
Soaking in the sunset
Setting a spreading fire
To glittering wave caps cresting
The distant indigo horizon
Recalling the last moment
Your eyes filled mine
The last words that tumbled
From trembling lips
To dance in awaiting ears
A sound
A phrase
Three words ablaze
Je t'aime cheri

Neither dreams nor miles
Can separate us now

Healthy Reminders

Breathe deep
Inhale the surrounding essence
And let it crowd your lungs

Stretch out
Unfold your limbs in the starlight
And bathe in the silver glow

Listen
Reflect on the auditory sensation
Of these lilting melodies

Live

Musings on Revelation and Reality

Started with a whisper
Ended in a shout
Every inch of my being
Electrified and burning
Engulfed in the holy flames
Of His purifying spirit
Cleansed and reborn
Fully alive in an instant
That started with a whisper
And ended in a shout...

Debating the Man in the Mirror

Shattered illusions
Interrupted the Monday doldrums
Currently occupying these scattered thoughts

Never would have guessed
This stark reality is what you'd prefer
That such bitter pessimistic futility
Brings more comfort
Than the warming hope
Of the unknown light

Staring reflection gazing out
Disbelief and exasperation evident
Wondering where the reset button is
And how it might all be undone

Misguided Saviour Complexes and My 15 Minutes of Fame

Smoke rises from the ashen remnants
Of all that ever was
Charcoal tendrils curling serpentine
Swaying in the volcanic breeze
A lonely dirge the only sonic interruption
Left to soothe these auditory nerves

I burned myself out
Reduced to a pile of molten slag
Trying to warm that glacial wall
Your heart remains within

Realization dawning far too late
Not my love
You really needed
It's not my place
To save

Lessons never savored
Or ever truly learned

Elm Street, Pre-Nightmare

The sun finally retreated
Sunk beneath the endless horizon
Surrendering the evening
To the fleeting whims
Of the lazy autumn moon
Gently sliding
Across the ebon sky

Flashing stars peek through
A shimmering gilded canopy
Beckoning all the children of the evening
To quit their nests and dens
Venture out into the waiting night

I wandered east on Elm
Drawn and tempted toward
What Springsteen called
"The darkness on the edge of town"
A thousand bad ideas
Just beneath the surface
And I sadly entertained them all

Dragon Awakening

Eyes alight on ascending spirals
Captivated by the rushing breeze
The pounding of massive leather wings
Beating humid air
Breaking gravity's iron grip
Diamond hardened scales rippling and glittering
reflecting the dying sun
Majestic
Resplendent
Utterly awe inspiring

Razor talons spring open
Steel trap in reverse
In all this ancient euphoria
It never once occurred to me
To fear this flight
Terror fully realized
Plummeting to earth

Headless Horseman and the Devil Band

Watched it rise
Palest golden orb in full display
Lunar waves spreading wide
Crisp illumination covering
This shadowed hallows eve

Lonely figures slowly fade into sight
Hollow phantasms long forgotten
Lost in the starving seas of time
Resurrected for their annual cemetery parade
Through the coveted domain of the living
Desperately trying to reclaim
Whatever passion consumed
Their earthbound former flight

March on, march on
Raise the chorus of the damned
Lift the banshee wail
And remind all the foolish living souls
Why they cling to every breath
Why every pumping drop of blood is precious
What it means
To truly be alive

All Saints Searching for the Dawn Patrol

Salt stings tired eyes staring at the sea
The pounding surf a lullaby
To soothe such savage nerves
Spent chasing silent phantoms
Awaiting midnight's icy embrace

Sizzling shafts of gold
Streaking across the violet horizon
To crack open November's inaugural dawn
Sending the shrieking spectral invaders
Scrambling asunder in contested defeat
At the onrushing triumph of Apollo

Moments From Surrender

"Tell me where it hurts"

Such a simple statement
Designed to elicit pointed conversation
Meant to serve as a healing catalyst
First step on recovery's winding road
Maybe even earnest self-evaluation

But what happens when the answer
Isn't simple
Doesn't have a preexisting condition
Or a standard execution method
What happens when what hurts
Is everything
Will you still be so willing
So eager
When every breath is agony
Every move is excruciating
And life is on the downside

Is it really love that drives you?
Is everything they say about you true?
Are you truly unafraid and unconcerned
By the horrors hiding within me?

"Yes...tell me where it hurts"

It's all Gonna be OK...Hope in the Aftermath

Reaching out in the shadows
I find myself dwelling in
Fingertips stretched and seeking
Guided by sensual voices
Responding to this ephemeral touch
Tracing every track-mark scar
Faded railway map covering my raging heart
Pausing on each ragged edge
Connected by sewing needles
Emergency staples
Rough muscle covering
Long forgotten wounds
Still tender in their memory
Fighting every urge to hide it away
Encase it in iron and concrete
Never to be seen again
Never to feel again

Fist wrapped tight and tugging free
Exposing every anxiety to the brilliance
Of the unknown and unexplored
Holding out this beating organ
Raw and vulnerable
One more chance to love
Like it's the first time
At the gate

Barstool Romeo Makes His Move

Never have to wonder
What secrets come to light
At the bottom of the whiskey bottle
The liquid flames sliding slowly down
To fuel the familiar fire
Found most Saturday nights
In this sleepy coastal town

Never have to wonder
Every glass inches closer
To deepest honesty
And obliterated inhibitions
Chipping away at these
Neurotic anxieties
Tying my tongue

Never have to wonder
But I just can't help myself

Turn the Page and Take it from the Top

Awake in the fall out
Clarity stinging the eyes
With all the details you never wanted
And tried so hard to look past
But straws met camels
Backs were broken
And the bridge is burning clean

Stepping out and forward
Unfolding in the breaking dawn
Morning glory personified
In this new beginning fragility
Reclaiming that spark
And staving off the delirious chorus
Of "it might have been"

Sunlight washes over
Illuminating all that could be
In the teeming potential
Sparkling behind your eyes
Electric and passionate
Flowing from all you are
In the new day that's gloriously upon you

Phantoms Looking for New Souls to Spook

Silver slashes of slender moonbeams
Dance across the empty side
Of this antique queen sized bed
Throwing shadows and imagined shapes
Of someone long since gone away
Lost to the siren song
That sweetly calls us to our final rest

The spirits rise
Alight in the evening's chill
Dancing through their temptations
Screaming their hollow rage
Straining at the tethers
Binding them to limbo's embrace

Poltergeists and phantasms
Tired specters and silent ghosts
They all visit me in turn
Desperately seeking
A frightful dividend return
Disappointment abounds

The only thing that's truly haunting
Is your eternal memory
And the shadows that spark remembrance
Of you slumbering beside me

One-sided Conversations on Repeat

So much, it seems, just feels enormous
Great weights suspended in awkward ascent
The proverbial grand piano on a thread
And they're being raised in unison
By a juggling behemoth
Intent on tossing me in

All these enumerated anxieties
Well known and sadly familiar
In their sickening dread
Long shadows stretching over crawling hours
Intent on a final coffin call

Pinpoint in the distance
Flickering flame beckoning me to come
To leave behind the incarcerating cocoon
And find escape never thought possible
In the solitary valley of the dead

It might be folly
But the answer
Can only truly begin
By taking the first step

Christmas Carols and Silent Nights

Snow stirred reflection
Whispering in the winter wind
Amid the twinkling starlight
And the heated wassail aroma
Enveloping the festive celebration

So many memories flood the mind
Bringing silly smiles
Poignant tears
And a few new earnest wishes
Nestled 'neath the mistletoe

Walking out into the frigid night
Following that famous star
Thumbing down to Bethlehem
Seeking Heaven's king
And singing hallelujah

Conversing in Alien Tongues

Feels like millennia have idled past
Languid in their ebb and flow
Since the moment undeniable realization
Erupted in Vesuvian epiphany

I lost myself in the aftermath
Tempting the wrath of Oceania
With vague ambitions of being found
Suspended in the depths of Atlantean dreams
And a kingdom ascending

Feels like millennia
...And then you spoke in such florid delicacy
That time stopped altogether
And the universe stood in rapt attention
Waiting for the final revelation
To begin

An Afternoon Abroad

Shades of the lonely sentinel
Coloring Wednesday's outlook
On the oncoming storm

Wondering just what daybreak
Will rectify in the rising solar heat
And the dream of Spring's approach

It's only Thursday
And I'm just a fool in the rain
Longing for the sun beams
Singing Friday I'm in love

This Just In - You're Mortal! Mere or Otherwise...

Perched on the precipice of opportunity
Gazing over unknown winding pathways
Stretching into the twilight darkness
Enveloping the edge of all there ever was

Breathing in the overwhelming essence
Of an impending slow descent
Into the atmosphere of aurora valley
And the presence of idle temptations

Alive is not a guarantee
Of absolutes or best decisions
Or even clear concise directions
You get one any one of us gets
A solitary lifetime
To live
To love
Make it count and jump

Sunbeams Dreaming of Snowflakes

Released into the hazy winter morning
Hanging aloft in the crisp icy breeze
Flowing over fur and feather
Leaving crystalline reminders
Of chill reflection
As I freeze in the pale sunshine
Illuminating ivory sheets
Enveloping the outstretched plains
Unfolding into the disappearing horizon

Seconds split and strain
Shattering the mental hourglass
Suspended between moments
Entranced by the never-ending
Overzealous thought parade
Dreaming of plural singularity

Alive in the endless dichotomy

Next Stop, Black Diamond Eclipse

The sky cracked and yawned
Unleashing fluid ramblings
From heaven's maw
Encapsulating charcoal tinged landscapes
Now marrow soaked in alien ideologies
Running in torrential rivulets
Overwhelming the barren banks
Framing Charon's river vessel
Bound for Limbo's lonely shores

Just another rainy Wednesday afternoon
In the valley of the damned

Love in the Healing Light

Frozen in moments that span decades
The stifling hush of ignorant conformity
Enveloping malformed worldview designs
Painting shallow rigid frames of reference
Meant to brush away unknowns and anomalies

...But light has a funny way of creeping in
Spilling into cracks and forgotten crevices
Seeping through long held defenses
Gently radiating luminescence
Until confrontation cannot be ignored
And the shades snap open
Exposing every darkened fear
Uncovering guarded secrecies
Thought to be certain damnation

...And then the scales fall away
Sight revealed in virgin beginnings
That the light is not interrogation
Or oppressive subjugation
But the overwhelming warmth of a love
Pursued with relentless abandon

This is what Happens when the Brain is in Charge...

I wanted nothing more than to say that there
Was never any part of this that mattered in
The slightest bit and that every single moment
Spent in your company was just an aimless distraction
To pass the idle time on my hands
Until the ideal vision finally passed before
And pulled me out of these imaginary doldrums
To live in complete and utter bliss in the perfect
Sanitized fairytale happily ever after
But the solitary truth of all this strikes
The deepest nerves throbbing in the back of my calloused thoughts
And cuts down to the mental marrow
Eliminating every bullshit excuse ever uttered
To illuminate the shining realization
That I would never find anything more perfect
Than the moments in your arms
And the intoxicating taste of your kiss
That forever lingers on my lips
And I'll spend the rest of these sleepless nights drowning
In cheap bourbon and burning through every lonely muse
That can't hold a candle to the one I thought would never matter
Now permanently emblazoned in the flesh of my shattered heart

No Seriously, I've Mastered This One...

Placid azure surfaces stretching out
In twisted winding ribbons
That reflect the silver lunar waves
Glittering in languid currents
Gliding silently abroad
With an unnamed solitary purpose

Floating along
No other direction in mind
But the mercy of the stream
Wondering just what that means
To the man who craves
Undeniable absolute control
And is only in this very moment
Realizing the complete illusion
That entails

Never really have been anywhere
Done anything
This river didn't lead me to
Freedom in acceptance
Sweet release in letting go

Thoughts of a Foolish Heart

We are birthed with an undeniable inclination
Towards a completely selfish preservation
Of every notion making us central
To the universe's continued existence
And elevating our own importance
To paradoxical levels with associated complexes

Anything else would require an admission
Of responsibility towards more than just
Our own designs and machinations
Would mean that all these contrary thoughts
Are more than simply unevolved ideals

Still it seems we would rather sink
Into the yawning ebony decay
Content to drown in our own time
Than to ever acknowledge
An outstretched hand
And a healing light

Drive Thru Confessionals and Sea Worthy Saints

So many things I wanted to say in the dwindling span
Of circuitous seconds slipping between ragged breaths
Escaping from aching lungs collapsing under pressure
Retrieved from the sweet embrace of looming eternity
And the wide eyed stare of mislaid immortality
Swept away in the rising tides that wash me free
Of all my most treasured misconceptions
Leaving only salt stained sepulchers
And ashen monuments to fallen responsibilities
Long overdue for recompense

So many things...uninspired to sublime...but the only
Words that tumble free...I'm sorry...I'm sorry...

Mea culpa...mea culpa...mea maxima culpa...

Spaceshipwrecked on the Outskirts of Alpha Centauri

Cascading silver symmetry aligned
In oscillating troughs and waves
Crashing against shimmering opal shores
Awash in ancient maritime remnants
Rediscovered with the alternating tides
Seeking to reclaim the effervescent seas
Deep within the bowels of a rival kingdom
Hoarding this liquid paragon
That can be contained no more easily
Than the invisible winds buffeting
This makeshift survival shell

They knew this crash was an inevitability
The moment I lost control of a tempest
Raging at the heart of this stolen vessel
Knew I'd be marooned and alone
At the mercy of an alien landscape

No predictions were forthcoming
No prophecies to be sung
Only sudden death and rebirth
In the dangerous beauty of it all

Something Along the Lines of Self-Surgery in the Dark

Introspection comes calling unannounced
On these solitary spring evenings
Filled with humming cricket songs
That serenade my languid outlook
Peering into this shadow shrouded forest

Gradually they begin to appear
Glowing in the lunar waves
Glittering in piercing pairs
Slicing through my empty facades
Marching into inquisition
Replaying every interaction
In microscopic slow motion review
Giving birth to new anxieties
With their own idiosyncrasies
Distracted in reverie

Try a little self-reflection they said
It will be enlightening they said

And like Pandora I learn the futility
Of trying to replace the lid

Chameleon Colours for Spare Change

Swallowed whole by the interpretation
Resurrected in the manifestation

Sifting through the glacial decay
Cautiously plucking obscure rhythms
On invisible soulstring vibraphone keys
That reverberate in secret harmonies
And orchestrate this metamorphosis
Inevitably marked for adolescence

Swallowed whole by the interpretation
Resurrected in the manifestation

A summer lost in sullen silence
Enveloped between two existential auras
Enshrouded beneath enlightenment
Hoping for the valley
Not the locomotive
When the tunnel finally ends

Swallowed whole by the interpretation
Resurrected in the manifestation

Secret Language Decoder Ring Material

Fading into the storied pages
That line these dusty notebooks
Fallen to disuse and fraying disrepair
A shoddy relic of another age
Forgotten in the passing years

Once
Oh once there was a time
A night couldn't end
Until a familiar scratching pen
Stained ink on paper
Between leather bound covers
Ongoing chronicle
Recorded in secluded silence

It's all empty now
Fluid script replaced
By digital clicks
Soulless ambient glow
Illuminating weary eyes
Capturing keystrokes in bits and bytes

Dear diary
No longer you and me
The night never ends now
No new days to remember

...And It's Worth Saying Too...

There's something to be said
For the absent sound of silence
In the face of the always open mouth
Spilling verbal homicide
In every direction
Intent on breathing murder unsolicited
Into every life it touches
Under the guise of progress
Excising the very nature of freedom
In favor of a cheap imitation
Easily controlled
And forever manipulated

Yes it may be silence in the moment
But we're far from submission
And surrender is a foreign concept
In a war we've already won

Mixtapes and Other Forgotten Art Forms

Even in the deepest recesses
Of fully lucid dreaming
I tend to find myself the eternal auslander
Searching for the doorway to belong
And the golden moment that fades into you
With all the stolen rapture
Of intoxicating alien delights
Yet the only signal slipping through
Echoes the devastating symphony
Of destruction pulsing in exponential waves
Of inertia creeping in sonic obliteration
Until there's nothing left but swirling dust
And in that moment I am reborn empowered
With every waking adulation
Streaming from avian choruses
That greet this pale new dawn rising

Overactive Imaginations and Stereo Daydreams

I guess I was supposed to be scared
Frozen in anxiety and self-doubt
At the mention of anything related to you
And the possibility of things beyond
The current state of affairs
Where we never seem to match up or meet
And the only sound between us
Is the crescendo of crashing heartbeats
Mostly mine
Every time you pass this way and hesitate
Like the same scenario
Is dancing in your head
Keeping you up long into the night
With questions and what ifs
And other silly dreams
But it's all projection
Misdirection
Overactive romanticism
Beaming from my consciousness
Aiming for your closed circuit imagination
In the vain hope you might just feel it...

You stopped and smiled

I guess I was supposed to be scared
Congratulations I'm completely terrified

I Never Plan for the End of Anything at the Beginning of Everything

In the dusk of existence
When all the clocks have unwound
And the streaming seconds have drifted away
Into the awaiting timeless eternity
The memory banks begin to flicker and fade
One last 70 millimeter highlight reel
Rolling behind exhausted eyes
The veritable 'this is your life' montage
We so often seem to dread
Beneath the imagined weight of a finale
Outside of our own choosing

The moments fly past
Each a realization of impact
Never long held in their inception
But hindsight breeds clarity
And everything we thought useless
Now seems an essential treasure
In the grand telling
Of the unrivaled masterpiece
That is our story

The song slowly shimmers
The band plays a lullaby
But the dancefloor is empty
And the party is nearly over

I Prefer the Sundays, but You get My Point

Frozen

A typically gradual occurrence
Accelerated by the proximity
Of my life to your presence
In a truly remarkable fashion
Where the breathing stutters
The heartbeats stall
And the tongue sticks
While every second bleeds an eternity
Between clicks

Transfixed in the warmth of your gaze
The subtle curve of your lips
Curled in a mischievous smile
As exploratory fingers entwine in my own
And in that moment
I know I mean every word Mick ever sung
About wild horses and never letting go

Standing on the Shoulders of Gnats

Stopped in the present moment
Breathing in the onrushing night
Eyes transfixed on the awakening heavens
As my mind drifts off into curious thoughts
Of spiral galaxies and shrouded nebulae
Cloaking universal mysteries
In the dust of streaking comets
And the dying light of fallen stars

The moment flutters past
Leaving only the impression
And enormous implications
A certain mythic insignificance
In the face of gaseous giants

...And yet this overwhelming sense of purpose
Has never been more terrifically real before now

Reinventing Radio Revolution

The sound sidles slowly
Ambling in gentle waves
Oratory octaves oscillating
Clinging to the space between
Expanding existential erosion
Destroying boundaries within
Juxtaposed jocular journeys
Enveloping this headspace
Binaural audio intervention
Salvation in three chords
Whispered withered wilderness
Divinity in every listen

Summer Nights and a Quiet Light

A dream of years long past
Summer and seventeen
Strawberry Wine on the stereo
And the overwhelming intoxication of you
Invading every sense I possess
The stars never burned so bright
As the flame that danced between us
And no time will ever erase
The power of the moment
We first said hello...

Polaris

Shimmering pinpoints
Flickering in the twilight
The briefest of reminders
For the stars that were moments
Shared in midnight's embrace
Cold rays ancient and fading
In the wake of our gaze
Stretching through lifetimes
Unseen and undeterred
Steadfast and predestined
Illuminating the yawning darkness
Burning through eons
And falling to ash
In the atmosphere
Beckoning wishes
And contemplation
Amidst professions
Of undying love and devotion

Not Just Any Dream Will Do

Flying in a blue turtle dream
Languid through the motionless mentality
That permeates my thoughts
Rejuvenates my bones
Blossoms in a budding rest long deferred

Reflections in the quiet stillness
Awaken renewed resolutions
And spark the dormant kindling
Of passionate flames

The dawning of this glorious purpose
Far from the reaches of burden
Vitality in the secret of the easy yoke

About the Author/Contact Info

David Greshel is a Mississippi-born, Florida-bred author and poet with a penchant for music, movies, and all things pop culture. Never one to shy away from self-reflection and evaluation, he channels it all into his writing with the results you now see before you.

David currently resides in Palm Bay Florida and can often be found at live music events when not working, writing, or spending time with friends and family.

This is his second collection of poetry. His first collection, Windows into the Past for the Camera Shy, is also available everywhere.

Connect with David:

Email: dgreshel217@gmail.com
Facebook: facebook.com/david-greshel
Instagram: @electricinfamy
Twitter: @electricpoet217
Website: www.neonsunrisebooks.com

www.ingramcontent.com/pod-product-compliance
Lightning Source LLC
Chambersburg PA
CBHW031357040426
42444CB00005B/328